YOU AND ME SAVING THE SEA

by Courtney Lang

I would like to thank:

⭐ *Aquarium of the Pacific for allowing me to photograph some of their amazing exhibits*

⭐ *Jason Naudé for teaching me how to edit photos and taking two of the mermaid photos*

⭐ *Patagon Dive Center in Saint Thomas; Divers Down in the Cayman Islands*

⭐ *My Dad for diving with me and posing for the bike picture*

⭐ *My Mom for helping to transform me into a mermaid and the taking photos of me*

⭐ *My readers, for all the great things they will do to help our planet!*

I'm about to take you on an underwater adventure! Living under
the sea is so much fun! There are always new sights to see
and new areas to explore! Every time I explore a reef, I learn
something about our beautiful ocean. There are so many things
that most people (and mermaids) don't know about the deep blue
sea, so put on your swimsuit and get ready to dive in!

Did you know that 25% of all marine life lives on reefs, including thousands of types of fish?

Did you know that although coral looks like a plant or a rock, it's actually an animal?

Did you know that coral is related to jellyfish and anemones?

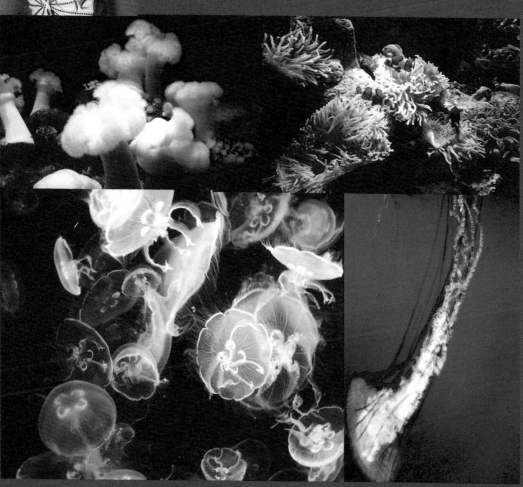

Did you know that coral reefs are home not only to fish, but also to sharks, crabs, eels, lobsters, and many other animals?

Did you know that there are many types of coral in all shapes, colors, and sizes? Some reefs are 10,000 years old!

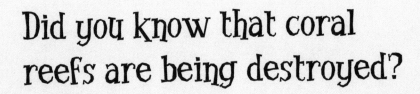

Did you know that coral reefs are being destroyed?

Healthy coral is beautifully colored. When it's sick, the coral turns white as if it were mixed with bleach. This is called coral bleaching. The temperature of our planet is getting warmer. This process is called Global Warming. Some coral reefs are dying because the ocean water is getting too hot for them. Coral reefs also are hurt by POLLUTION and changes in the environment.

Litter pollutes our ocean.

Boats sometimes drop
their anchors on reefs,
crushing the coral.

13

Too many trees are being cut down, causing EROSION. Erosion makes dirt fall into the ocean, which kills the coral.

14

Some fishermen poison
the water to catch fish.
This stuns the fish,
so they float to the
surface of the water
and are easier to catch.
The poison left in the
water ruins the coral.

INVASIVE SPECIES such as Lionfish are eating too many fish which is hurting the reef's ECOSYSTEM.

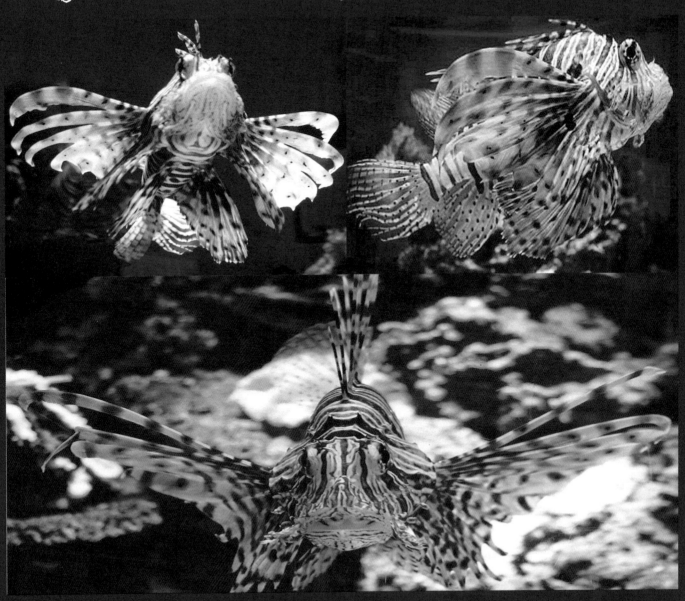

There is too much carbon dioxide in the ocean. This is called OCEAN ACIDIFICATION. This is a big problem because when there is too much acid, it slows the coral's growth and weakens their fragile skeletons.

Some boats use fuel that pollutes the water.

Although there are tons of fish in the ocean, too many fish are being caught. This is called overfishing. It is hurting the ocean's ecosystem.

You can help!

Recycle cans, cartons,
glass, plastic, and paper!

You can help by throwing away trash.
Litter sometimes drains into the ocean.

WARNING
RUNOFF/STORM DRAIN WATER
MAY CAUSE ILLNESS
AVOID CONTACT WITH PONDED OR
FLOWING RUNOFF AND THE AREA WHERE
RUNOFF ENTERS THE OCEAN

AVISO
CORRIENTE DE AGUA/AGUA DEL DRENAJE DE
TORMENTA PUEDE CAUSAR ENFERMEDADES
EVITE CONTACTO CON AGUA DE DESAGÜE QUE
ESTE ESTANCADA O CORRIENDO Y EL AREA
DONDE DESEMBOCA AL OCEANO
ORANGE COUNTY ENVIRONMENTAL HEALTH DIVISION
FOR FURTHER INFORMATION, CALL (714) 667-3752

Drink from reusable water bottles.

Take shorter showers. A shower uses about 2 1/2 gallons of water per minute! Water is a limited NATURAL RESOURCE and we need to CONSERVE it.

Recycle EWaste!
EWaste is anything that uses
batteries or needs to be plugged in.

25

Try to carpool or ride your bike.
I like to swim!

Don't waste water!
Turn off the faucet
while you are
brushing your teeth.

Plant a tree!
This helps the Earth's ATMOSPHERE.

Bring your own reusable bags to the grocery store.
Plastic is polluting the ocean. There is a Texas-sized giant mass
of trash swirling in the middle of the ocean called the Great
Pacific Garbage Patch. We don't want it to get any bigger!

Turn off the T.V., lights, and computer to save energy when you are finished using them. Deep in the sea, there are fish that are BIOLUMINESCENT, which means they make their own energy and glow in the dark. They don't ever turn off!

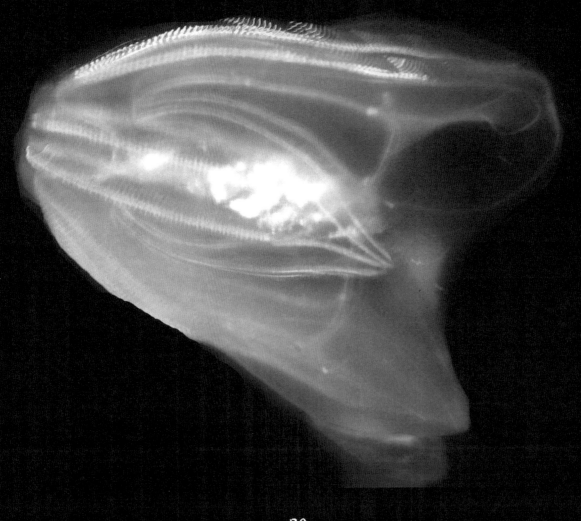

Properly dispose of HAZARDOUS WASTE. When this kind of waste gets into the air, water, or land, it can spread harmful chemicals that damage the health of the ENVIRONMENT. Luckily, solving this problem is easy: make sure to properly empty all containers before throwing them away.

We can work together to make a healthy planet!

GLOSSARY

ATMOSPHERE – gas and other particles surrounding the earth as well as other planets

BIOLUMINESCENT – plants and animals that can make their own light

CONSERVE – to protect or save

ECOSYSTEM – interactions between plants, animals, and their environments

ENVIRONMENT – physical surroundings that affect the plants and animals that live around them

EROSION – what happens when the earth's surface is worn away by the action of water and wind

HAZARDOUS WASTE – something that is damaging to the environment and harmful to humans and other living things

INVASIVE SPECIES – harmful types of plants or animals that do not naturally live in a specific area

NATURAL RESOURCES – materials that are helpful to certain plants or animals, including humans, such as water, sunlight, wood, and food

OCEAN ACIDIFICATION – when too much carbon dioxide (CO_2) is in the ocean

POLLUTION – action of making the planet unclean with man-made waste

To do research and take photographs for this book, I went scuba diving extensively in the Caribbean Sea, off the coast of California, and the Great Barrier Reef in Australia. I visited aquariums and beaches. Besides personal visits, I have gleaned valuable information from books and Web sites. The following resources helped a lot:

Miller, G. Tyler, and Scott Spoolman. *Living in the Environment, AP Edition*. 17. Belmont: Brooks/Cole, 2012.

"Best Practices - Saving Reefs Worldwide." *Reef Check - Saving Reefs Worldwide*. N.p., n.d. Web. 3 Aug. 2012. <http://reefcheck.org/conservation/Best_Practices.php>.

"Coral Reefs: Threats." *WWF*. N.p., n.d. Web. 3 Aug. 2012. <http://wwf.panda.org/about_our_earth/blue_planet/coasts/coral_reefs/coral_threats/>.

"Global Warming." *National Wildlife Federation*. N.p., n.d. Web. 04 Aug. 2012. <http://www.nwf.org/Global-Warming/Effects-on-Wildlife-and-Habitat/Coral-Reefs.aspx>.

"Great Barrier Reef @ Nationalgeographic.com." *Great Barrier Reef @ Nationalgeographic.com*. N.p., n.d. Web. 03 Aug. 2012. <http://www.nationalgeographic.com/ features/00/earthpulse/reef/reef3.html>.

Johnston, Ian. "Study: Plastic in 'Great Pacific Garbage Patch' Increases 100-fold." *World News*. NBCnews.com, 9 May 2012. Web. 04 Aug. 2012. <http://worldnews.nbcnews.com/_news/2012/05/09/11612593-study-plastic-in-great-pacific-garbage-patch-increases-100-fold?lite>.

"Ocean Acidification: The Other CO2 Problem." *Ocean Acidification*. N.p., n.d. Web. 08 March. 2012. <http://www.nrdc.org/oceans/acidification/>.

"Questionnaire #3How Much Is Your Daily Indoor Water Use?" Water Science Questionnaire #3: Water Use at Home. N.p., n.d. Web. 04 Jan. 2012. <http://ga.water.usgs.gov/edu/sq3.html>.

"Why Care about Coral Reefs? | Coral Reef Alliance." *Welcome | Coral Reef Alliance*. N.p., n.d. Web. 3 Feb. 2012. <http://www.coral.org/resources/about_coral_reefs/why_care>.